SUNRISE
SENTIMENTS
Morning Inspirations & Reflections

WILLIAM L. McLEOD
and KEVIN T. McLEOD

PUBLISHING

HOV Publishing a division of HOV, LLC.
www.hovpub.com
hopeofvision@gmail.com

Cover Design: Hope of Vision Designs
Editor/Proofread: B. Walker Consulting

Contact the Author, William and Kevin McLeod at:
mcleod.kiana@gmail.com

For further information regarding special discounts on bulk purchases, please visit www.hovpub.com

ISBN Paperback: 978-1-942871-85-9
ISBN eBook: 978-1-942871-86-6

10 9 8 7 6 5 4 3 2 1

Printed in the United States of America

Dedication

I dedicate this book to my son Kevin who has always been a constant blessing in my life. I thank God for bringing such a soul into my world. May you accomplish all you set out to achieve and fulfill the path God has created for you. Keep your eyes on God, and you will not fail. For what God has intended for you, NO ONE can take away.

You are blessed. You are loved. You are and always will be a child of God and my son.

SUNRISE
SENTIMENTS

Morning Inspirations & Reflections

Contents

SUNRISE
SENTIMENTS

Morning Inspirations & Reflections

Introduction

When I was first approached to write this book the first thought that came into my mind was, "It's about damn time." You see, I had mixed feelings about the relationship between me and my father. Based on the last four decades, I would describe our relationship as inconclusive. I say this because as far back as I can remember, my dad and I had the most loving father-son relationship and human connection one could ever imagine. I would hug my dad and kiss him. In my mind, there was nothing strange about the love and affection I expressed towards my dad because I did not know anything different.

My conjugal family, which consisted of my mother ("ma"), my father ("dad"), sister Keeva and myself, were a very closely-knit family. Particularly, when it came to our connection and sense of reassurance as a family. In many ways, our family dynamics probably seemed a bit surreal compared to the experiences of the families living around us. When I was younger, my dad was always actively involved in my life. A point of view my mother frequently disagree with. However, in my novice male perspective and point of view, I saw things differently. The fact that my dad was physically present and emotionally available in my life was something a lot of my friends never experienced. A fact, I apparently took for granted until it was brought to my attention later in life.

The intent in bringing it to my attention was never to embarrass me or make me feel less than. It did, however, make me feel a bit awkward in that I felt as though I had been branded as some normalized outcast in the community. The truth is, most of the families within our community were so broken, disjointed, and disconnected that a lot of my friends did not have fathers or father figures to look up to. As such, many of them had a warped perspective when it came to love and relationships.

Most of my friends lived vicariously through the interactions and relationship I had with my dad, often looking up to my dad as their dad too. So, in addition to my one biological half-brother, I gained quite a few "stepbrothers" who voluntary and involuntary developed a relationship with my dad through a constant and stable connection with me. The fact that I acquired all these stepbrothers was something I had not given much thought to until my early to mid-30's. With that said, this book is an expression of my sentiments to my dad—a man who like the sun that faithfully rises and sets every day—became a father, husband, and friend to so many. The man who birthed and ignited my very existence and the love I have for my own sons.

SUNRISE
SENTIMENTS
Morning Inspirations & Reflections

An Open Letter to My Father

Kevin T. McLeod

Dad, I love you. Despite all our experiences, both good and bad, there could never be another to replace you. You are one of a kind William McLeod—Will, Bill, Cool Hand Luke, Sensi, Mr. McLeod, Old Man—or whatever they are calling you there days. LOL. We have had play fights and real fights, both verbal and physical. We have had bailouts and let downs. I appreciate you dearly for allowing me to participate in this project of sorts, which has propelled me into greater journeys of exploration.

I had absolutely no desire to write a book, though the thought had crossed my mind on a few occasions. The drive simply was not there to execute it. However, the thought of a collaboration between one cool dude and another younger cool dude, ignited a spark in me that led to this metaphorical road trip between the two of us!

As a youngster, I was extremely playful and loving. That part of my personality has never changed. As I continue to grow and mature through family fun, fights, new additions, and separations, the spirit that drives the love between us has never diminished. In a world that is defined and revolves around the person I am today, all I can say is my fly-by-night behavior has been enriched and enlightened because of you.

And yes, I admit there have been a few times when I erupted from a state of calmness. Like the time my uncle supposedly and accidentally stabbed mother in the hand. (Don't ask). Do you remember how in the heat of the moment, I suppressed my rage despite your obvious and inevitable anger? You taught me that.

Do you remember how I used to beat you up on the regular, as mother, sister, and I remained reigning kings of the sneak pillow fight attacks? Nothing but distance has changed the dynamics of our love and relationship.

Do you remember how, to this day, we still swap jokes on the phone dissing each other just to keep each other sharp? Do you remember that time, Mr. Cool, when you drove your bus to the front of my high school, as a part of your routine stops, saw me on the outside and asked what was I doing outside the school? And how, after telling you I had been kicked out of class, your demeanor never changed? I still remember your infamous response, "I'll talk to you when we get home."

These are some of the things I think about as I reflect on the relationship we share and the joys of having a dad like you!. Love you homie!

Morning Inspirations

William L. McLeod

In latter part of 2018, I began sharing some morning inspirations on social media to encourage both believers and non-believers, and to build and develop their faith and relationship with God. These inspired writings became the sole basis and content of *Sunrise Sentiments: Meditation and Reflections.* To follow are some of the inspired thoughts that will, hopefully, expand my outreach to others and serve as an introduction to my son Kevin, the book's co-author:

Morning Inspiration – Day 1

Good morning! The sun is shining and there's plenty of light. A new day is dawning sunny and bright. How do I know? Because God woke me up. So, rise, shine, and give God all the glory! Lift your voice and say, "So glad I'm here! So glad I'm here, in Jesus' name! Oh, glory!" Praise God for His faithfulness and abundant grace and mercy. Praise God for the great things He has done. Hallelujah!

Morning Inspiration – Day 2

Good morning! Father God, in the name of Jesus, I pray for all those in need of prayer. Those in nursing homes, hospitals, or at home. I pray that God heals them all and place angel's all around them and their families. Show them the abundance of Your mercy and grace. Touch their bodies and show them your awesomeness. Thank you, Father, in Jesus name. Amen.

Morning Inspiration – Day 3

Good morning! God woke us up today to see the light because He is the Light of the world. Go out into the world and wherever God takes you, shine. Praise God, great things He has done. Hallelujah!

Morning Inspiration – Day 4

Good morning! Lift your voice to God. Get up and go to a church that teaches the gospel of the grace of Jesus Christs, because this is the day that the Lord has made. I hope you'll rejoice and be glad in it. Praise God. Hallelujah!

Morning Inspiration – Day 5

Good morning! You are about to have one of the biggest days of your life. How do I know? Because God woke you up and he has a purpose for you. Go out into the world and let the light of Christ in you shine. God be with you.

Morning Inspiration – Day 6

Good morning! Awaken today in peace and with a sound mind. No matter what happens in life, Jesus is your comfort, peace, and an ever-present help in trouble. Praise God for His comfort and peace. Praise God for the great things He has done. Hallelujah!

Morning Inspiration – Day 7

Good morning! I'm blessed to have a family who's rooted in the word of God, recognizes His voice, uses good judgment, and applies Godly wisdom. Thank you, Jesus, for the foundation that you established for me and family. We are blessed. Thank you, Jesus, for the great things You have done. Hallelujah!

Morning Inspiration – Day 8

Good morning! No matter what we are going through, we are washed by the blood of Jesus. Keep the faith and remember that we are children of God. Trust Him because He will never fail us. He loves us and has shown His love for us through His sacrifice on the cross. What we're going through is a test of faith. Trust God. He will bring us through and protect us. Praise God, for the great things He has done. Hallelujah!

Morning Inspiration – Day 9

Good morning! When life is not going the way you want, when nothing you do seems to make sense, and you feel you have no hope, trust in the Lord Jesus Christ. In times of trouble Jesus will always throw you a rope. Thank you, Jesus, for the great things You have done. Hallelujah!

Morning Inspiration – Day 10

Good morning! Watching the news about Covid-19 and how it's affecting the world. I'm trying to figure out what God is trying to tell us. I believe that God is telling the world to repent, get baptized, and prepare for the coming of the Lord Jesus. He's coming back again soon. Praise God, for the great things He has done. Hallelujah!

Morning Inspiration – Day 11

Good morning! Lately I've been looking back on the last 63 years of my life on earth, and everything that has happened within that time. God has always brought me through. So, why would I stop trusting Him now? Corona virus you are defeated. You have no power or authority here because I have been washed in the blood of Jesus Christ. Trust God and use Godly wisdom. Praise God, for the great things He has done. Hallelujah!

Morning Inspiration – Day 12

Good morning! There is no turning back because I've come too far from where I started from! Despite what's going on in the world, I choose to trust the One who created all things. Praise God, for the great things He has done. Hallelujah!

Morning Inspiration – Day 13

Good morning! Thanking God for the abundance of his grace and mercy. I am a child of God! God is telling me to be still and know that He is God. Trust in the salvation of the Lord. I choose to trust Him in all things, including the Corona virus. Why? Because He is God. Praise God, for the great things He is doing. Hallelujah!

Morning Inspiration – Day 14

Good morning! Looking at the world's reaction to Covid-19 and the panic it's causing. I am a tree planted by the water and I shall not be moved. Why? Because Jesus Christ is my Lord and Savior. No matter what happens, I choose to trust Him. Hallelujah!

Morning Inspiration – Day 15

Good morning! Our God is a good God! Oh yes, He is! Our God can do everything. So, trust Him through the storms, sunshine, and rain. Do not panic. He will deliver. Be still and watch the salvation of the Lord. Praise God, for all the things He has done. Hallelujah!

Morning Inspiration – Day 16

Good morning! In 2 Timothy 1:7, Paul wrote that God does not give us a spirit of fear, but of power, love and a sound mind. No, we are not to fear. We exercise Godly wisdom. God's wisdom is telling me to stay home and pray. Thank you, Jesus, for Your wisdom. Praise God, for the great things He has done. Hallelujah!

Morning Inspiration – Day 17

Good morning! I truly believe that through the storms, rain, heart aches, and pain (and even the Corona virus), God will bring us through it ALL. Thank you, Jesus! Isaiah said, "No weapon formed against us shall prosper." (Isa. 54:17). Praise God, for the great things He has done. Hallelujah!

Morning Inspiration – Day 18

Good morning! I awakened to a new day. Counting my blessings. Learning from past lessons, praising God for this life, and not taking anyone or anything for granted. I'm asking God to direct my path and order my steps in His Word. Despite what's going on in the world, I trust God. He woke me up today, and He did the same for you. So, get up, and let God use you for His purpose. Praise God, for the great things He has done. Hallelujah!

Morning Inspiration – Day 19

Good morning! Thanking God for everything He provides to the world. The sun gives us light and energy. The air provides oxygen to keep our body's functioning. The rain waters the earth and allows the harvest to grow. If anyone thinks there is no God, then I would say, "Wake up! Look at God's wonders!" Praise God, for the great things He has done. Hallelujah!

Morning Inspiration – Day 20

Good morning! I'm taking no one and nothing for granted today. Jesus didn't take us for granted when He woke us up this morning. I'm thankful for the Light in the world because I see nothing but beauty. Yes, I'm praising God and letting Him know how grateful I am! Praise God, for the great things He has done. Hallelujah!

Morning Inspiration – Day 21

Good morning! Knowing what I know about Jesus now, I wouldn't want God to change a thing. I look back at my life and all the storms, disappointments, heart aches, and pains. If I had to do it all over again, I wouldn't change a thing because life has taught me to appreciate God through every storm. Hallelujah!

Morning Inspiration – Day 22

Good morning! Walk by faith and not by sight. Let your talk be your walk, keeping in step with God's word and instructions for you. Believe in God's word and trust Him, for He makes no mistakes. Amen.

Morning Inspiration – Day 23

Good morning! As I reflect on my childhood and being raised in Harlem, NY, I recall the vivid memories of playing on the basketball court and other enjoyable moments of my childhood. My life was not perfect, but it was uniquely mine. Thank you, Jesus, for the childhood I experienced. It greatly influenced the man I am today. Amen.

Morning Inspiration – Day 24

Good morning! It's a beautiful day in New York City. The sun is shining bright. The temperature is around 56 degrees. Spring is in the air. The birds are singing and everything God created is at work. You and I are a part of that. Stay focused and do not stray. Allow God to use you for His purpose and will. Praise God, for the great things He has done. Hallelujah!

Morning Inspiration – Day 25

Good morning! God woke me up this morning with my mind set on Jesus. Thank you, Jesus, for another blessing. To see a new day is a blessing and I choose not to complain. Give God all the glory, honor, and praise. Go out into the world and do God's work, whatever that may look like for you. Praise God, for the great things He has done. Hallelujah!

Morning Inspiration – Day 26

Good morning! Life is so beautiful when you cast all your burdens on God. Jesus carried a heavy cross for our sins. He died on that cross for you and for me. Thank you, Jesus! Hallelujah!

Morning Inspiration – Day 27

Good morning! Woke up early this morning thinking how much I've been blessed. Blessed with the ability to see, touch, smell, hear, and taste. Something so simple and yet so influential to my life. Take a moment and just thank God for what you have. You may not have everything you want but you have everything you need. Thank you, God, for keeping us and continuously providing for us. Praise God, for the great things He has done. Hallelujah!

Morning Inspiration – Day 28

Good morning! At home talking to God and thanking Him for all He has done and all that He has provided, not only for me but the entire world. He withheld his wrath, extended His mercy, and gave us His grace. I'm so thankful Jesus went to the cross! Praising God, for all the great things He has done. Hallelujah!

Morning Inspiration – Day 29

Good morning! Life is magnificent. Life is beautiful. Life is amazing. Life is precious. Life is a gift from God. Enjoy the beauty of the gift of life that God has given us. Praise God, for the great things He has done. Hallelujah!

Morning Inspiration – Day 30

Good morning! When God calls one of his children home, why do we say, "Rest in peace?" 2 Corinthians 5:8 says, "To be absent from the body is to be present with the Lord." If we are a part of God's kingdom, are not we already at rest and peace? Food for thought. Amen.

Morning Inspiration – Day 31

Good morning! The difference between religion and Christianity is, Christianity is not a religion it's a lifestyle and walk with God. Hallelujah!

Morning Inspiration – Day 32

Good morning! There is something about the name of Jesus. His name is all power. His name is all knowing. His name is mercy. His name is mightier than anything we can think of or ask for. His name brings life. His name is a strong tower. His name is unconditional love. I can't think of another leader who can make these claims. Praise God, for the great things He has done. Hallelujah!

Morning Inspiration – Day 33

Good morning! Jesus loves you. He paid a debt that He didn't owe. He did it, just for me and for you. That's love. Praise God, for the great things He has done. Hallelujah!

Morning Inspiration – Day 34

Good morning! In life, there will be many thunderstorms, rain showers, stormy, and sunny days. Regardless of the weather, always remember you can still shine. Why? Because Jesus Christ, the Light of the world is in you. His light outshines any storm you can imagine, even those you cannot see. He is always shinning. Amen.

Morning Inspiration – Day 35

Good morning! You are about to have one of the biggest days of your life. How do I know? Because God woke you up and he has a purpose for you. Go out into the world and let the light of Christ in you shine. God be with you.

Morning Inspiration – Day 36

Good morning! Looking at the sky with its beautiful shades of blue and white. Everything appears to be in order and at peace. Just wondering if God was trying to tell us that our lives should be at peace and order. Food for thought. May God be with you.

Morning Inspiration – Day 37

Good morning! God woke me up with my mind on a specific message. We need to know how Christ lived, so we can know how we are to live. Christ lived a life of unconditional love. "As long as we are at home in the body we are away from the Lord." (2 Corinthians 5:6). Thank you, Lord. Thank you, for our inheritance in Heaven where there is total peace and love. Hallelujah!

Morning Inspiration – Day 38

Good morning! Looking back and thinking about what God has brought me through. Through all the hardships and storms in life, I've learned to trust Him and be obedient to His Word. God didn't have to do what He did for me and my family. He did it because of love. Thank you, Jesus, for loving me and my family. Hallelujah is the highest praise we can offer You. I am so grateful and thankful that You went to the cross just for me. Praise God, for the great things You have done. Hallelujah!

Morning Inspiration – Day 39

Good morning! As we express our love for others, let's not forget the One who loved us so much, He gave His life for us. There is no greater love then this. Hallelujah!

Morning Inspiration – Day 40

Good morning! Just a reminder that every day is a day to acknowledge the special people God has place in your life. Let us be mindful of this every day of the year. Hallelujah!

Morning Inspiration – Day 41

Good morning! What if God had not gone to the cross? Where would we be? What would we be? How would we act or react? What would be our thoughts? Who would comfort us, teach us, and guide us? I'm not sure. All I know is I am so grateful He did. Thank you, Jesus, for going to the cross. Thank you, Jesus for the great things You have done. Hallelujah!

Morning Inspiration – Day 42

Good morning! What a wonderful surprise I got this morning. God opened my eyes and I saw light. I know that tomorrow is not promised. For that reason alone, I live everyday as if it is my last. I'm giving my flowers to you today, right now, at this very moment. I know that Jesus loves you. Praise God, for the great things He has done. Hallelujah!

Morning Inspiration – Day 43

Good morning! On this rainy New York City day, I am reflecting on how much I use to complain about the rain. That is, until I realized without rain nothing would grow. Rain is God's way of cleansing, purifying, and watering His creations so everything can continue to grow and survive. Hallelujah!

Morning Inspiration – Day 44

Good morning! As each day goes by, I learn to appreciate the air that I breath, the visions I have, and the ability to feel smell, touch, see, and hear. I'm learning not to take the abilities I have for granted and to enjoy life in abundance. Thank you, Jesus, so much for these abilities. Praise God, for the great things He has done. Hallelujah!

Morning Inspiration – Day 45

Good morning! Thinking about what I've done to deserve Jesus' love for me. Why would He provide for me and my family? Why did He protect us through the dangers, hardships and pains of life? Why did He heal all our wounds? Why did He pay a debt He didn't owe, just for me and you? Why? Because He loves us. Give God all the glory, honor, and praise! Let Him know how grateful you are. Thank you, Jesus, for Your love. Hallelujah!

Morning Inspiration – Day 46

Good morning! A day older. A day wiser. Another opportunity to right a wrong. Another day to see my family and friends. Another day to go out into the world and enjoy the wonders of God's creation. I choose to get up and take advantage of the blessings of God. Why? Because He woke me up to see another day. I'm so grateful and thankful for his unconditional love. Thank you, Jesus, for the great things He has done. Amen.

Morning Inspiration – Day 47

Good morning! Just thinking about the goodness of God and how He's provided for me and my family over the years. I realize, my biggest blessing is my redemption and new life in Christ. I have an inheritance and I'm seated on the right hand of the Father with Jesus Christ. Thank you, Jesus, for the great things You have done. Hallelujah!

Morning Inspiration – Day 48

Good morning! I'm up early, relaxing and thinking about how much God loves me and my family. Despite what we've been through, God has been so very good to us. Praising God for his unconditional love. Hallelujah!

Morning Inspiration – Day 49

Good morning! You cannot add nor subtract from the word of God. God makes no mistakes, but people do. Something to think about. Thank you, God, for your faithfulness. May God be with you.

Morning Inspiration – Day 50

Good morning! Woke up this morning with a peace of mind, no major health issues, no worries, no major concerns, food in the kitchen, bills paid on time, and heat to keep me warm. I have a positive outlook on life and God lives in my heart. What more can I ask for? Thank you, Jesus, for the great things You have done. Hallelujah!

Morning Inspiration – Day 51

Good morning! Sometimes when God wakes me up, I don't always want to get up. However, I still get up because I know God woke me up on purpose. He has a purpose for me. Praise God, for the great things He has done. Hallelujah!

Morning Inspiration – Day 52

Good morning! The love of Jesus Christ is greater than any power known to man. It's called resurrection power. The same power that raised Jesus Christ from the dead. Hallelujah!

Morning Inspiration – Day 53

Good morning! Don't be ashamed of God, because He is never ashamed of you. Go out into the world and share the gospel of Jesus Christ and do it boldly. Hallelujah!

Morning Inspiration – Day 54

Good morning! When God woke me up this morning all I could think of to say was, "Thank you, Lord! Thank you, Lord! I just want to thank you Lord." Hallelujah!

Morning Inspiration – Day 55

Good morning! Thinking about the past and all that I've been through. I realize that when I wasn't walking with God as a result of disobedience, God was still walking with me. Thank you, Jesus, for your faithfulness. Hallelujah!

Morning Inspiration – Day 56

Good morning! What a beautiful and magnificent day. God woke you up in the light to see His light. So, get up, go out, and walk in the light of Christ, the Light of the world. Hallelujah!

Morning Inspiration – Day 57

Good morning! Trouble is all around us. Storms come into our lives. No matter what your conditions or circumstances may be or how you may feel, remember Jesus Christ is still Lord and He can do all things. Hallelujah!

Morning Inspiration – Day 58

Good morning! This Christian life we live is only difficult when we try to live it apart from God. If we let go and get out of God's way, walking with God is not complicated. Hallelujah!

Morning Inspiration – Day 59

Good morning! Thinking about how blessed I am to have such wonderful family, friends, co-workers, and church family. I am blessed to have been taught by a man of God who, not only teaches us what we want to hear but what we need to hear: The gospel of God's grace. Thank you, Jesus, for such a blessing. Amen.

Morning Inspiration – Day 60

Good morning! When God who is our Father speaks, listen very carefully. His word is power, truth, and can move even the biggest mountain. How do I know? Because our God is God all by Himself. No one compares to Him. Hallelujah!

Morning Inspiration – Day 61

Good morning! When you look back over the years—remembering all the tears, all the fears, all the rights and wrongs, good and bad—remember that through it all God brought you through. Praise God, for the great things He has done. Hallelujah!

Morning Inspiration – Day 62

Good morning! I've tried to accomplish many things in life and each time I failed. I thought success boiled down to how well I prospered in the flesh. I took credit for what God had done until I discovered success is not what you accomplish on your own, but rather what you accomplish through God. Amen.

Morning Inspiration – Day 63

Good morning! Whatever situations you may endure in life, good or bad, turn to God. He will always be there for you 24/7, 365 days a year. Amen.

Morning Inspiration – Day 64

Good morning! Jesus is the Light of the world. The light of Christ overrides darkness. Don't walk in darkness because it will cause you to take the wrong road in life and stumble and fall. Walk in the light of Christ and you'll never make a wrong turn. Amen.

Morning Inspiration – Day 65

Good morning! Regardless of our current circumstances, we have a God who can do all things. He will bring you through. Spend time with Him in prayer. He loves you and wants you to talk to Him. You know his number. He's always available and you'll never get a busy signal. Hallelujah!

Morning Inspiration – Day 66

Good morning! The sun is shining and there's plenty of light. A new day is dawning, sunny and bright. How do I know? Because God woke me up. So, rise, shine, and give God the glory. Praising God for his faithfulness and abundant grace and mercy. Praise God, for the great things He has done. Hallelujah!

Morning Inspiration – Day 67

Good morning! It's a beautiful day in the neighborhood. No matter how bad things may be, if you look at life the way God looks at us, you'll realize how great life is. Give thanks to God for giving us a new day. God pours out his grace, mercy, and love upon us. Give God the praise and be grateful for the great things He has done! Praise God. Hallelujah!

Morning Inspiration – Day 68

Good morning! No matter what's going on in your life, no matter how bad you feel, what you've done wrong, what your history is, what your present conditions or circumstances are, Jesus still loves you. He loves you unconditionally, without prejudice or finding fault. How do I know? Because He died for us and set us free from eternal condemnation. We are now free to be all that God says we are. Don't stop praising God. Don't stop worshiping God. No matter what you're going through in life, remember God holds you close and will never let you go. Praise and worship God, no matter how you feel. Keep the faith. Praise God, He will never let us go. Amen.

Morning Inspiration – Day 69

Good morning! I just hit the biggest lotto in history! God woke me up. Some things in life you can't put a price on because they're priceless. Hallelujah!

Morning Inspiration – Day 70

Good morning! It's a new day, new blessings, and new miracles. If you have not accepted Jesus Christ as your Lord and Savior, don't wait. Tomorrow is not promised to any of us. Amen.

Morning Inspiration – Day 71

Good morning! Come one, come all. Let us gather around to hear about a Rock who laid his life down. A Rock that is more precious than gold. Come hear the greatest story of love story ever told. There was a man from Galilee, performing miracles for every eye to see the goodness of his mercy and grace. He so loved the world that He left a Heavenly place to come to Earth. No, He didn't beam down. He simply came by birth. With all power and authority, Jesus took the place of sin for you and me. If God had not died on the cross, we all would be lost. Thank you, Heavenly Father, for sparring no cost. The greatest act of love is when Jesus went to the cross. Hallelujah!

Morning Inspiration – Day 72

Good morning! What a beautiful morning! It's a beautiful day. The sun is shining bright in New York City. The cold winds are blowing, and God is shining bright upon us. We are blessed and highly favored of God. Hallelujah!

Morning Inspiration – Day 73

Good morning! What a beautiful day in the neighborhood. Just enjoying the beauty of life. Yes, God is so good. We are blessed to see this day. Thank you, Jesus, for the great things you have done. Hallelujah!

Random Thoughts

Random Thoughts

Kevin T. McLeod

Random thoughts are mentally captivating outbursts that have yet to become verbal. As my mindset naturally evolves artistically, I often experience scatterbrain thoughts that consume me. To follow are a few of these sporadic thoughts of randomness:

* * * *

I remember dad cashing his paycheck at a money van located on the inside of his bus depot. Whenever I was with him he would give me a two-dollar bill, which I cherished for many years to come. However, I eventually spent them. To this day, I keep a small stash of the memory in my memory.

* * * *

Prior to attending the *Golden Gloves* boxing tournament at Madison Square Garden, a few of dad's coworkers would stop by a local convenience store for some snacks and a few scratch off tickets. Everyone, including me, had a ticket but mine was the only one that won! I was only 12 years old back then and had just won my first $30 Lottery Scratch Off Ticket!

* * * *

I remember riding the bus with my dad while he worked as a bus driver for the Manhattan Transit System (MTA). I enjoyed every minute of it! From the long M15 bus routes to the long enjoyable lunch breaks with dad on a bus all to our own. The experience exposed me to the various neighborhoods and cultures of New York that I had never seen before.

* * * *

I was about 10 years old when I had my first impromptu fight. My mother had sent me to get some bread from the store, located just outside of our apartment building. On my return, one of the boys in my building smashed the bread. My mom sent me back downstairs with my dad to exchange the loaf. The boy tried smashing the bread again in addition to hitting me, right in front of my father. My father instructed me to hit the boy back, but I was so angry I actually pushed and kicked the boy down the steps. LOL.

* * * *

My father and I would do cycling tours and fitness runs together.

About the Author

William L. McLeod was born and raised in  Harlem, New York on 134th street. He attended P.S. 175, followed by *Louis D. Brandeis High School* in New York City. Shortly after graduating, he enlisted into the United States Army. Prior to his enlistment, he met Ruth Artis-McLeod. Not long after his discharge from the Army, he and Ruth married and started a family. Together, they have raised three beautiful children: Kevin, Keeva, and Kiana. William's grandmother, Hazel Elizabeth McLeod, was the first person to introduce William to Jesus Christ as a young boy. Whenever she attended church, which was often, she would always take him with her. William eventually left the church during his teenage years to explore life on his own terms, which resulted in him experiencing a number of deeply personal trials and tribulations. In 1982, he gave his life back to Christ as a result of his wife joining *Beulah Baptist Church* in Harlem. Devote members of the church, William and Ruth raised all three of their children with a solid belief and faith in God.

Kevin T. McLeod, William's youngest son was  born in Harlem but raised in the Bronx, New York. At the early age of 7, Kevin joined *Beulah Baptist Church* and gave his life to Jesus Christ. From his youth, Kevin exhibited a gift for the creative arts, attending the *High School of Art and Design* in Manhattan to develop his artistic skills. In 2015, Kevin married Fatima Newton and together have raised five beautiful children. As the co-author of this book, Kevin shares memories of his relationship with his father, William L. McLeod.

Morning Inspiration & Reflections Journal

Morning Inspirations_____

_____

_____

_____

_____

_____

_____

_____

_____

_____

_____

_____

*Morning Inspirations*_____

_____

_____

_____

_____

_____

_____

_____

_____

_____

_____

_____

_Morning Inspirations_____

_____

_____

_____

_____

_____

_____

_____

_____

_____

_____

_____

*Morning Inspirations*_____

_____

_____

_____

_____

_____

_____

_____

_____

_____

_____

_____

Morning Inspirations _____

_____

_____

_____

_____

_____

_____

_____

_____

_____

_____

_____

*Morning Inspirations*_____

_____

_____

_____

_____

_____

_____

_____

_____

_____

_____

_____

*Reflections*_____

_____

_____

_____

_____

_____

_____

_____

_____

_____

_____

_____

Reflections_____

_____

_____

_____

_____

_____

_____

_____

_____

_____

_____

_____

*Reflections*_____

_____

_____

_____

_____

_____

_____

_____

_____

_____

_____

_____

_____

Reflections_____

_____

_____

_____

_____

_____

_____

_____

_____

_____

_____

_____

*Reflections*_____

_____

_____

_____

_____

_____

_____

_____

_____

_____

_____

_____

_____

*Reflections*_____

_____

_____

_____

_____

_____

_____

_____

_____

_____

_____

_____

9 781942 871859